We will miss you!

This is a book of letters, notes, memories, and pictures to celebrate our favorite times with you.

A TRIP DOWN
MEMORY LANE...

share a memory...

share a memory...

_____

_____

_____

_____

_____

_____

_____

share a memory...

share a memory...

_____

_____

_____

_____

_____

_____

_____

_____

share a memory...

share a memory...

share a memory...

share a memory...

_____

_____

_____

_____

_____

_____

_____

share a memory...

share a memory...

_____

_____

_____

_____

_____

_____

_____

share a memory...

share a memory...

_____

_____

_____

_____

_____

_____

_____

_____

share a memory...

share a memory...

share a memory...

share a memory...

_____

_____

_____

_____

_____

_____

_____

_____

share a memory...

share a memory...

_____

_____

_____

_____

_____

_____

_____

share a memory...

share a memory...

_____

_____

_____

_____

_____

_____

_____

_____

share a memory...

share a memory...

_____

_____

_____

_____

_____

_____

_____

_____

share a memory...

share a memory...

_____

_____

_____

_____

_____

_____

_____

share a memory...

share a memory...

share a memory...

share a memory...

_____

_____

_____

_____

_____

_____

_____

share a memory...

share a memory...

_____

_____

_____

_____

_____

_____

_____

_____

share a memory...

share a memory...

share a memory...

share a memory...

_____

_____

_____

_____

_____

_____

_____

_____

share a memory...

share a memory...

share a memory...

share a memory...

_____

_____

_____

_____

_____

_____

_____

_____

share a memory...

share a memory...

_____

_____

_____

_____

_____

_____

_____

share a memory...

share a memory...

_____

_____

_____

_____

_____

_____

_____

share a memory...

share a memory...

_____

_____

_____

_____

_____

_____

_____

share a memory...

share a memory...

_____

_____

_____

_____

_____

_____

_____

_____

share a memory...

share a memory...

_____

_____

_____

_____

_____

_____

_____

share a memory...

share a memory...

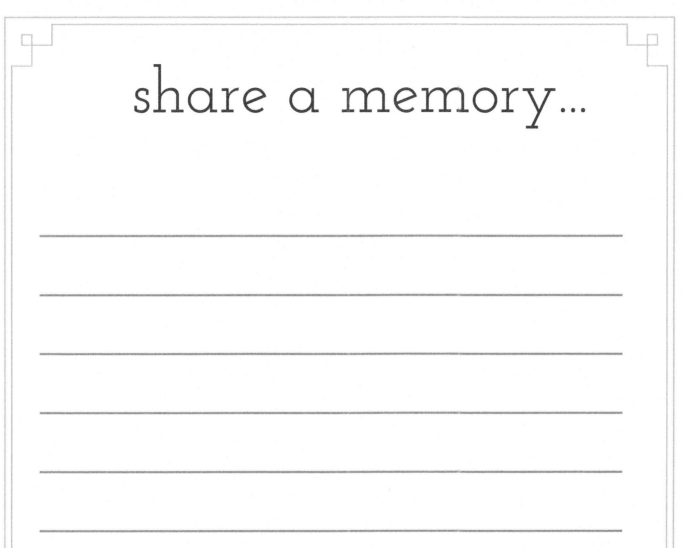

Made in the USA
Monee, IL
13 May 2022

96349184R00033